T0390103

SHIPS AHOY!
Dredgers

by Kaitlyn Duling

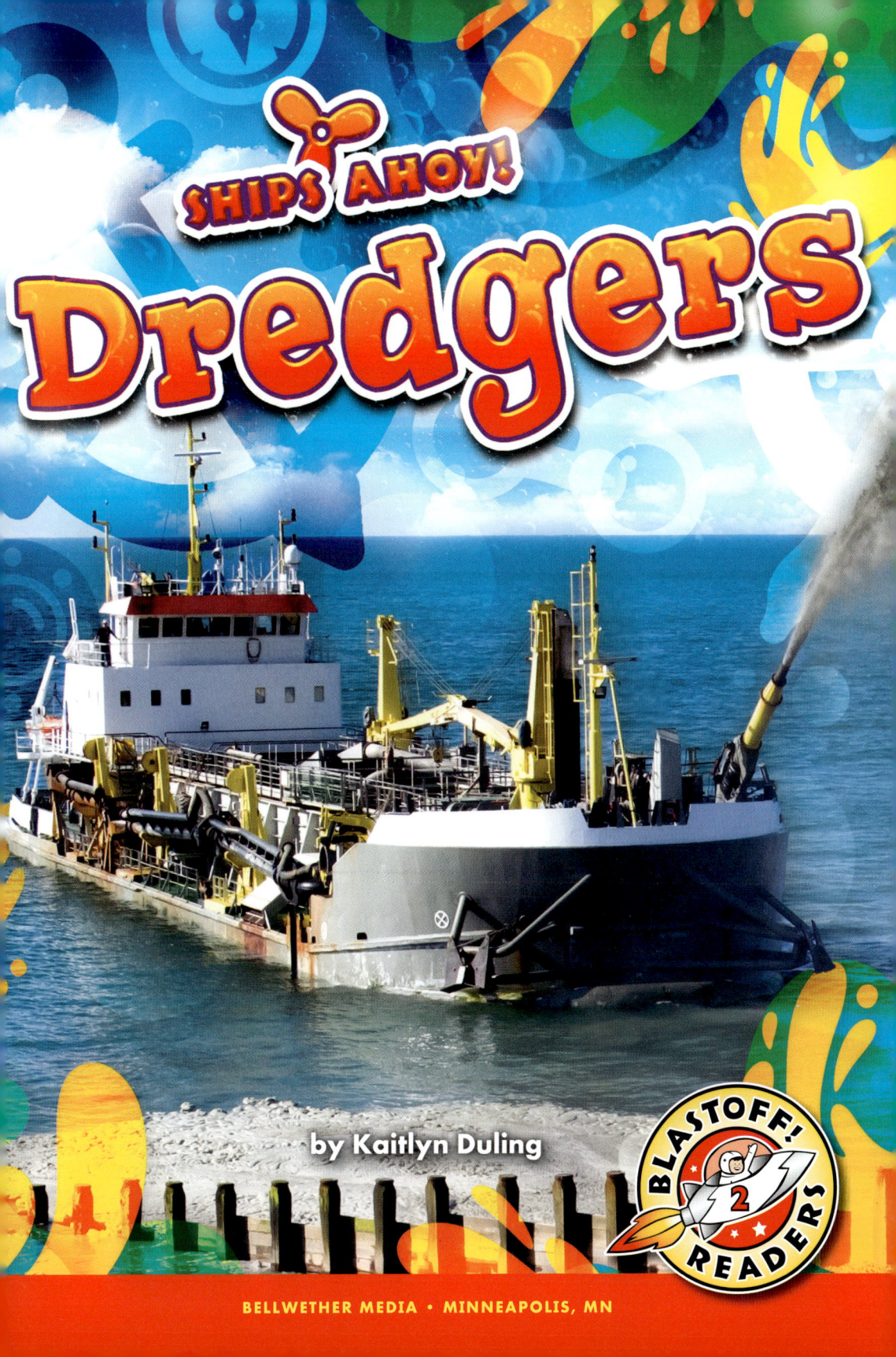

BELLWETHER MEDIA • MINNEAPOLIS, MN

Blastoff! Readers are carefully developed by literacy experts to build reading stamina and move students toward fluency by combining standards-based content with developmentally appropriate text.

Level 1 provides the most support through repetition of high-frequency words, light text, predictable sentence patterns, and strong visual support.

Level 2 offers early readers a bit more challenge through varied sentences, increased text load, and text-supportive special features.

Level 3 advances early-fluent readers toward fluency through increased text load, less reliance on photos, advancing concepts, longer sentences, and more complex special features.

★ **Blastoff! Universe**

Reading Level

Grade
K

Grades
1–3

Grade
4

This edition first published in 2026 by Bellwether Media, Inc.

No part of this publication may be reproduced in whole or in part without written permission of the publisher. For information regarding permission, write to Bellwether Media, Inc., Attention: Permissions Department, 3500 American Blvd W, Suite 150, Bloomington, MN 55431.

Library of Congress Cataloging-in-Publication Data

LC record for Dredgers available at: https://lccn.loc.gov/2025010686

Editor: Suzane Nguyen   Designer: Jeffrey Kollock

Printed in the United States of America, North Mankato, MN.

Table of Contents

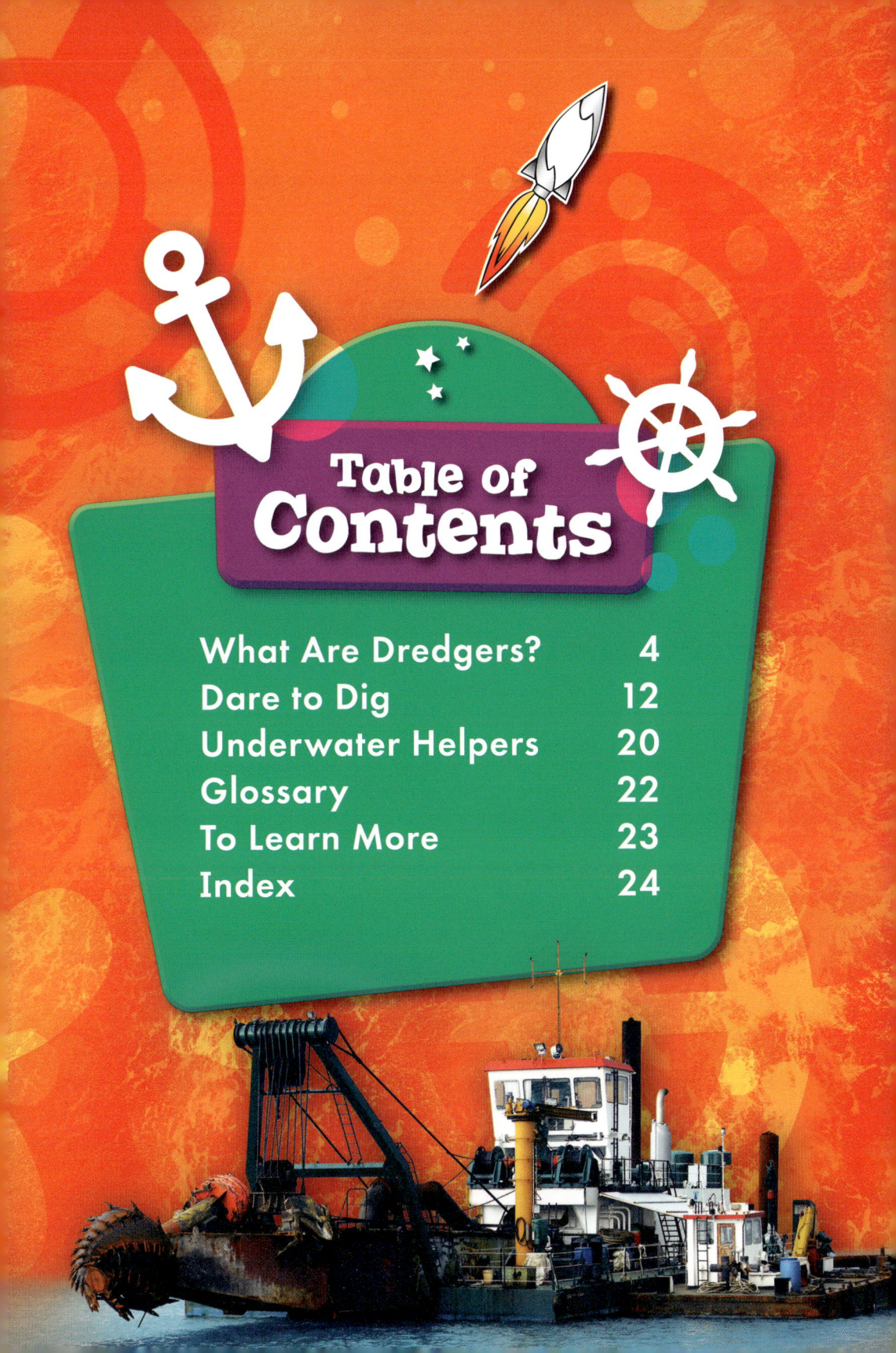

What Are Dredgers?

sediments

Dredgers are ships that remove **sediments** from bodies of water.

4

Dredgers clear waterways. Some are used for **mining**.

There are many types of dredgers. Some move with **barges**.

Others float on **platforms** to get work done.

dredger

barge

IAN BLANKEN

Bucket ladder dredgers have many buckets. They move down and up a ladder.

The buckets scoop rocks and soil. Then they dump them down a **chute**!

Parts of a Bucket Ladder Dredger

chute

buckets

ladder

Types of Dredgers

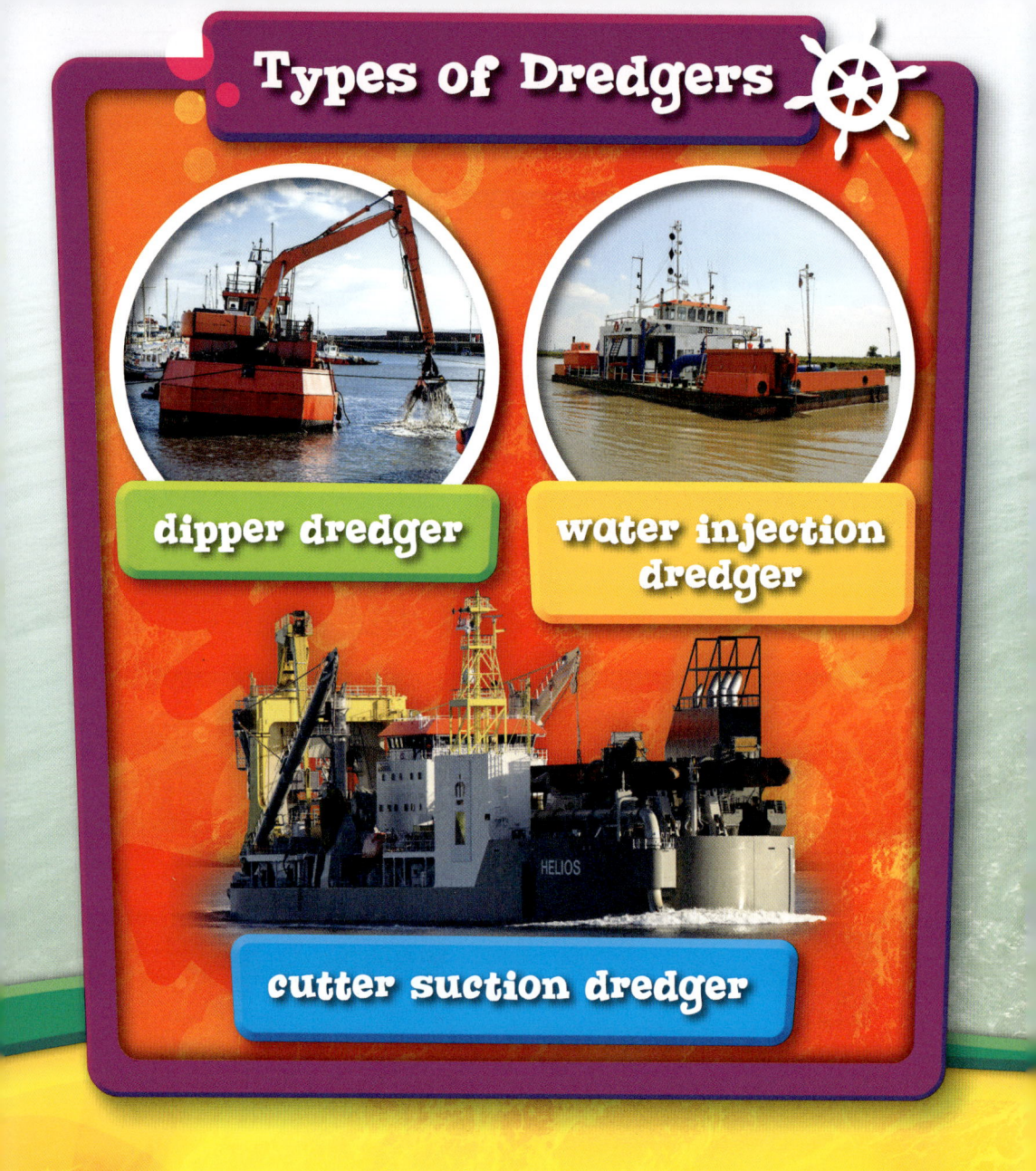

dipper dredger

water injection dredger

cutter suction dredger

Dipper dredgers use one big bucket to dig. Water injection dredgers spray water to remove sediments.

cutter

Cutter suction dredgers
break up sediments.
The dredgers suck them up!

Dare to Dig

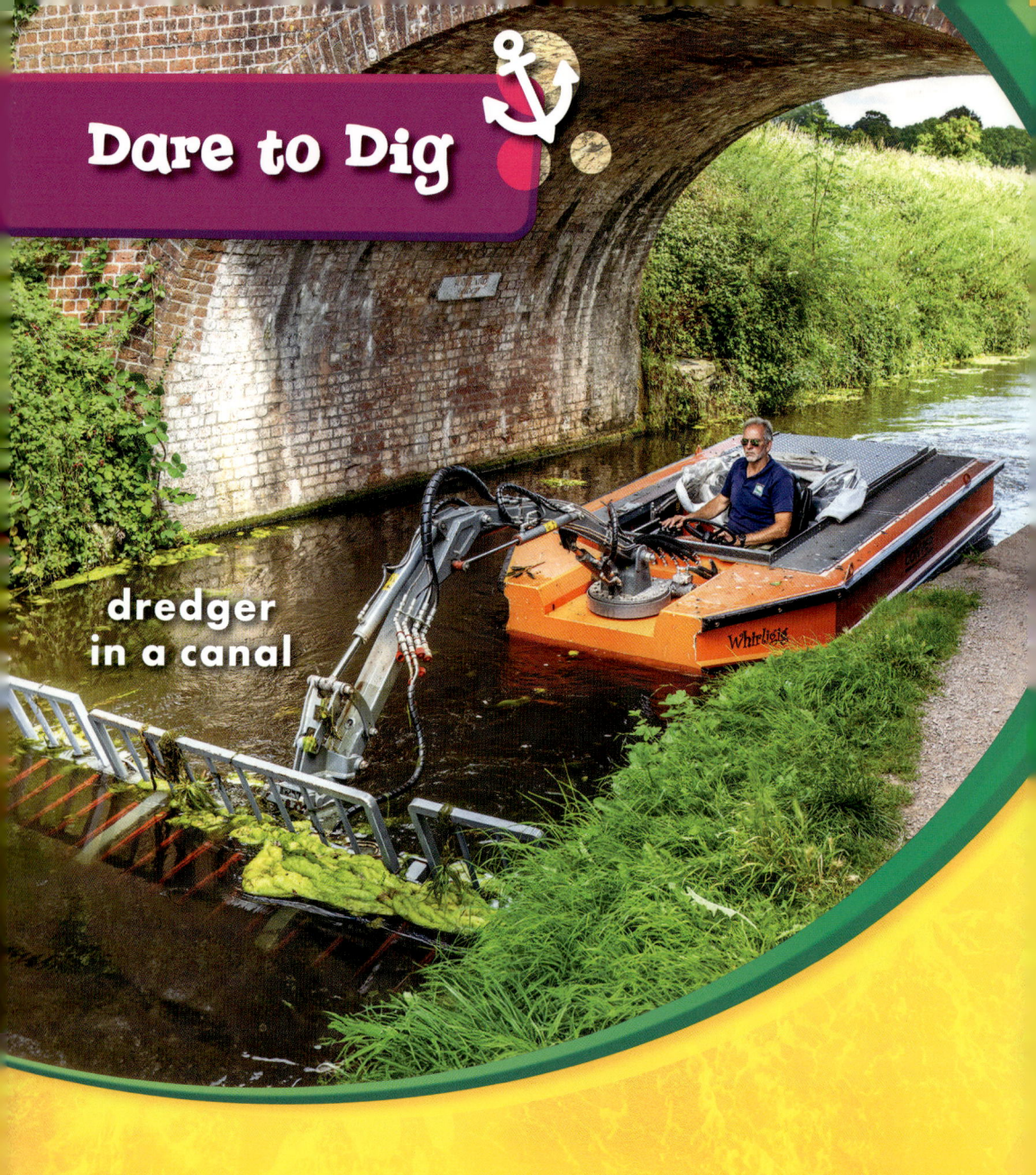

dredger in a canal

Dredgers are used in lakes, rivers, and **canals**. Some work on the ocean!

Dredgers must move slowly. Most travel around 2.6 **knots** (3 miles or 5 kilometers per hour) while they work.

Dredgers have dozens of workers. **Engineers** fix the dredger's **engine**.

Ship Stats

Spartacus

Size 538 feet (164 meters) long; 111 feet (34 meters) wide

Type cutter suction dredger

Top Speed 12.5 knots (14.4 miles or 23.2 kilometers per hour)

14

Purpose dredging deep underwater

welder

anchor

Welders fix the metal items like buckets and chains. Mates help drop and pull up the **anchor**.

15

control room

Dredge operators use cutters to break up hard rock.

Levers and buttons in the control room help them move the cutter.

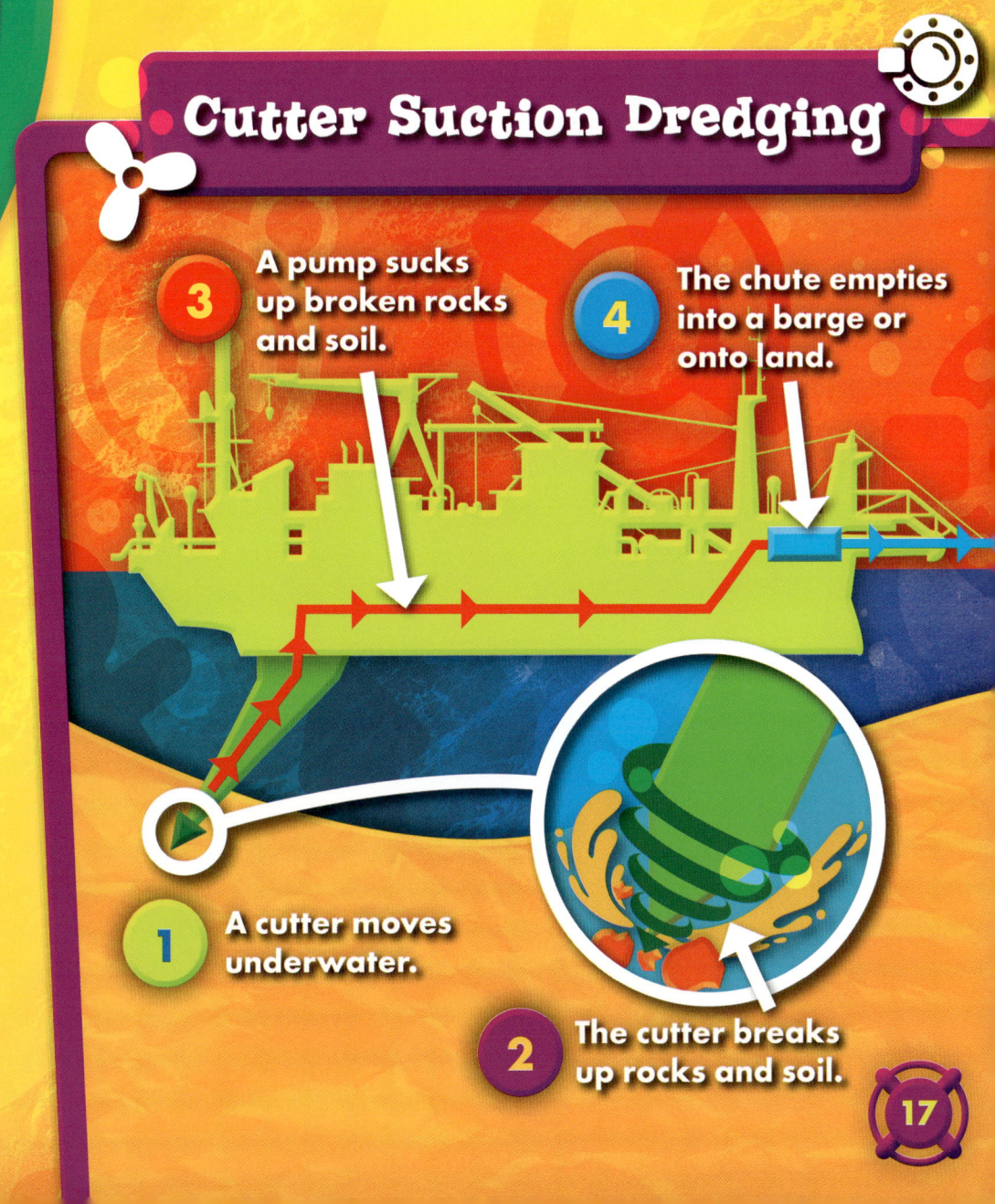

Cutter Suction Dredging

3 A pump sucks up broken rocks and soil.

4 The chute empties into a barge or onto land.

1 A cutter moves underwater.

2 The cutter breaks up rocks and soil.

Deckhands keep the dredger safe and clean.

deckhands

18

galley

Workers sleep in cots on larger dredger ships. They eat in the **galley**.

19

Underwater Helpers

Dredgers can help clean up water **pollution**. Dredgers also widen our waterways.

These amazing ships have many uses!

pollution

Glossary

anchor—a heavy object attached to a chain that sinks to the seafloor and keeps a ship in place

barges—long, narrow boats that are flat on the bottom

canals—human-made waterways that connect to other bodies of water

chute—a narrow tube that things go down or through

cutter—a rotating tool that cuts into rocks and soil

engine—a machine with moving parts that changes power into motion

engineers—people who design and build engines, computers, and other machines; engines are parts of machines that make them go.

galley—the kitchen on a ship

knots—units of measurement used to explain the speed of a ship

mining—the process of taking valuable materials out of the earth

platforms—flat areas where machines can work; platforms can be on ships or built in the water.

pollution—something that is harmful to the air, water, or land

sediments—tiny pieces of rocks, minerals, and other natural materials

To Learn More

AT THE LIBRARY

Duling, Kaitlyn. *Barges*. Minneapolis, Minn.: Bellwether Media, 2026.

Ruby, Rex. *Super Sedimentary Rock*. Minneapolis, Minn.: Bearport Publishing Company, 2025.

Schuh, Mari. *Diggers*. Minneapolis, Minn.: Bellwether Media, 2025.

ON THE WEB

FACTSURFER

Factsurfer.com gives you a safe, fun way to find more information.

1. Go to www.factsurfer.com.

2. Enter "dredgers" into the search box and click 🔍.

3. Select your book cover to see a list of related content.

Index